D1314516

FACT AND FANCY ABOUT THE FUTURE LIFE

Fact and Fancy About the Future Life

by

SAMUEL A. CARTLEDGE, A.M., B.D., Ph.D.
Professor of New Testament
Columbia Theological Seminary
Decatur, Georgia

RICHMOND John Knox Press VIRGINIA

6089-(1)-5324

PRINTED IN THE UNITED STATES OF AMERICA

To My Mother

REBECCA LAMAR POULLAIN CARTLEDGE

To My Mother

REBECCA LAMAR POULLAIN CARTLEDGE

TABLE OF CONTENTS

~~~~~~

PREFACE

~~~~~~

THE IMMEDIATE occasion for the writing of this volume was the request of the pastor of a large church for a book that could be put into the hands of church members to counteract some of the fantastic ideas that are being thrust upon them from so many sides in so many ways.

The author has sought to keep this request in mind throughout the book. He has striven for brevity and for simplicity. The reader is not supposed to be familiar with the intricacies of theological literature.

The author has tried to take a positive approach as much as possible, though at times it was necessary to present views with which he had to differ.

There are really three levels in the book. The first deals with those things which the Bible clearly teaches about the future. The second deals with some of the theories of Bible students which are used to try to explain those portions of the Bible that are not so clear and to fill in the gaps of the Biblical revelation. The last deals with some of the typical cults and isms that present teachings that are out of harmony with the Bible as interpreted by the scholars of the church down through the ages. The matters dealt with in the first level are, of course, by far the most important.

<div align="right">S. A. C.</div>

Columbia Theological Seminary
Decatur, Georgia

CHAPTER ONE

INTEREST IN THE FUTURE

~~~~~~

LONG, long ago the fact of death became a part of human experience. Abel was a vibrant, active personality. Then he became a cold, lifeless corpse. Soon his body became a part of the very dust of the earth. We may be sure that the hearts of his parents, if not of his murdering brother, were torn with grief as they realized that they could no longer have their beloved son with them. And we may be sure that even that early they could not help wondering if death really were the last word in the drama of human experience.

The fact of death is with us still. We have all gathered around the open grave and seen the bodies of our loved ones given back to the earth. "Ashes to ashes, dust to dust." Each one of us realizes that he, too, may be laid below the sod. So for our loved ones and for ourselves we think about the mystery of the grave.

There is also a natural interest in the future of the world and of the universe. The present state of affairs has been in existence for many centuries and millenniums, but in many religions there is found the belief that this is not the final state. In Christianity there is the belief that Jesus Christ is coming back to earth, that He is going to separate between the good and the evil, that the good will spend eternity with Him in the new heavens and the new earth, and that the wicked will spend eternity in the place of punishment.

Naturally the Christian wishes to have a competent knowledge of the future. He wishes to know the basis for the beliefs of his creeds. He wishes to know how he may be certain of obtaining an entrance into the state of eternal blessedness. He is interested in ascertaining as much as possible about the hereafter. He wonders how soon the end may come, for himself and for the present age.

Where can the answer to all of these questions be found? From ancient times men have been using their own reason in seeking to supply the answers, and human reason has been able to throw some little light. But we all know that the minds of no two men work exactly alike, so we are not surprised to find many divergent conclusions reached. Then we all recognize that factors are involved that go entirely beyond human knowledge. No person now living has himself experienced the life beyond the grave, and no one of us is competent in his own right to predict the course of future events with anything more than a bit of intelligent guessing.

The Christian believes that God has seen fit to give a revelation of Himself and of some of His plans in Holy Scripture. God has graciously revealed at least a part of what is in store for us. What human reason was unable to ascertain, divine revelation has made known. Thus, for the Christian, Scripture is the primary source of information about the future.

There are those who consider the Bible to be simply a human book; they respect it as the product of the religious experiences of many good and worthy men. They do not, however, consider it in any sense a supernatural revelation from God. What the Bible says about the future is no more authoritative for them than their own conclusions and guesses.

The belief of historic Christianity, however, is quite dfferent. We recognize that God made use of human authors in recording His revelation, but the thing that makes the Bible unique is the divine superintendence over those human authors which made their work God's work also. This is not the place to give the proofs for the doctrine of the inspiration of Scripture, which may be found in the fuller works on systematic theology and apologetics. The author wishes to state at the outset his own firm conviction of the truth of the divine authority of Scripture. That belief will color this whole volume, for the book is being written by one believer in Scripture to other believers in Scripture. Our primary purpose is to unfold what Scripture itself tells us about the future.

But if God Himself has revealed in Scripture the things about the future, why is there so much difference of opinion among Bible believers about the future? There are many things in the Bible that are so simple and plain that even little children can understand them and be sure about them; there are other things that are so deep that the wisest of men have not been able to comprehend them as yet. At times the Bible speaks in simple, matter-of-fact prose; at times it makes use of all kinds of figures of speech. At times the Bible gives no information whatever about points that may be of interest to us, so we have to fill in the gaps hypothetically for ourselves.

We are all aware of the fact that numerous denominations have grown up within the Christian Church. The majority of these bodies agree in accepting Scripture as their divine authority. But most of the denominations have arisen because of different interpretations of Scripture. For example, some earnest Christians believe that the Bible teaches that baptism means immersion; others believe that it means sprinkling; others believe that both modes are perfectly Scriptural. It is not surprising, then, that there should be real differences of interpretation when we come to the Bible teaching about the future, especially when we recognize that the subject matter itself makes it almost inevitable that much figurative language be used.

We shall see that much of the Bible teaching about the future is very clear and certain. And we ought to recognize that part as the most important part; God has not left us in doubt about the things that really matter most. There is an area, however, in which honest, Bible-believing Christians are not able to reach complete agreement. Here it is perfectly legitimate to make use of theories in interpreting matters that are not perfectly plain, and in filling in the gaps between the matters revealed by Scripture. Theories must be used in all branches of knowledge; they do no harm so long as they are recognized as theories, and they may even be steps toward fuller knowledge. Christians may disagree greatly in their theories, but they should learn to disagree as friends.

There are, of course, all kinds of theories about the future. Some are quite plausible, while others go far beyond the bounds of reason. Speculation about the future has brought forth some of the most fantastic of theories along with the most reasonable. The intelligent Christian should seek to evaluate the theories with which he comes in contact. He should subject every theory first of all to the plain teachings of Scripture. Then he should search for the most reasonable interpretations for those passages that are not so plain.

It is not to be expected that all Christians will ever agree on all their theories. "For we know in part," even the great Apostle Paul had to admit. The intelligent Christian should learn the facts that the Bible presents to him. He should be aware of at least some of the reasonable theories, recognizing them as theories, and refusing to lose his love for those who may hold different theories from his own. He should know how to avoid those theories that go so far as to contradict Scripture itself or the plain teachings of human reason and experience.

The fact that some Christians have developed their fanciful, even fantastic, theories about the future has made many Christians believe that they would do well to leave the whole subject alone. In reality that fact ought to inspire us to find out what the truth actually is. There is not the slightest need for going into the realm of fantasy, as countless Christians will affirm.

The subject of the future is always of great interest to Christians, but in times of great crisis it takes on an added importance. Especially is this true in times of war. Many of our dearest friends are being brought face to face with violent death, so the question of what is in store for the individual after death becomes of vital interest. Then there is the belief expressed in many quarters that the war is a part of the events leading up to the end of this age and the beginning of a new and better one. Does Scripture have anything to say about this particular war and its relation to God's eternal plan for His universe?

The future is of interest to all of us because all of us must one day experience the future. But why not wait until that day before thinking about it? Scripture teaches us that we must prepare for the future if we expect to spend our eternity with God. Were it not for our belief in the future, all of us might well adopt the creed of the Epicurean: "Let us eat, drink, and be merry, for tomorrow we die." The Christian, however, should live in the light of eternity. He should gain all possible guidance, comfort, and inspiration from God's revelation about the future.

CHAPTER TWO

THE GRAVE IS NOT THE END

WHEN our loved ones breathe their last, we lay them tenderly beneath the sod. We know that they are taken away from us. We can no longer hear their familiar voices and have sweet fellowship with them in all the common tasks and joys of life. Our hearts are made sad as we think of facing the days ahead without those who have come to play such an important part in our own lives.

There are some who say that the grave is the end. And they are able to give some very plausible reasons to substantiate that conclusion.

They can say that no one of us has ever seen anyone come out of the grave. We have seen many bodies laid away, but we have not seen a single one come forth alive after death. So far as our own personal experience is concerned, death certainly seems to be the end.

There is force in that argument, but it is far from being conclusive. We cannot draw a universal negative conclusion from our own limited experience. No one of us ever saw George Washington, but that does not mean that such a person never lived. As we shall see, we have historical proof that at least one person has come out from the grave. But we should realize that normally those who come from the grave will not come back and share this kind of life with us; they pass into a life of the spirit that is very different from this life. Denying the reality of the life of the spirit is like a blind person denying the fact of light. No one of us has experienced that new life yet, but that does not give us the right to say that it does not exist.

Those who say that the grave is the end may seek the aid of natural science. They may claim that human beings are made up of certain chemical elements, such as hydrogen, oxygen, phosphorus, iron, sulphur, and so on. The scientist can take a human body and tell exactly how much of each element is in it. We may not be flattered when we are told that those elements are worth just about a dollar. Now, they say, when we die those elements separate and go back into the cycle of nature, and that is the end of us.

But is it? A scientist may take a body and break it down into those elements. But that scientist has no right to say that those elements comprise the totality of that person. Let him start with those elements. Let him put them back together and make a human body out of them. Let him make that body live. Let him give that body a mind, a character, a personality, a soul. When he has produced all of that from those chemical elements we shall be ready to listen to him when he says that those elements are all. The better scientists have given up completely the old materialistic philosophy; many scientists have never held to it. We may freely admit that our bodies are made up of matter only, but we have abundant evidence that we are more than just our bodies.

On the other hand there are certain intimations, even in the realm of natural science, of immortality. A plant may seem to die, but there is life in a tiny little seed that it leaves; and from that seed may come up another plant. A seed may be placed in the ground and seem to decompose completely, but there comes forth a great tree. In the mystery of human life, cells are passed on from generation to generation. There is the belief in the indestructibility of matter; even when an object is burned it is not destroyed but becomes simply other forms of matter and of energy. Then again, whether you believe in evolution or in progressive creation, you recognize that man is the crown of the whole process, and that it is not his body or even his life that makes him distinctive, but his human personality or his soul. The Creator finally produced that high product; is it reasonable that He meant for it to last only threescore years and ten and then come to an end, when we see so many signs of indestructibility in so many of the lower products of nature? Of course we recognize that these things are only intimations at best; naturally, the limits of physical science make it impossible for it to prove that there is such a thing as the immortality of the soul.

We may also recognize that philosophy gives its intimations of immortality. Philosophers have used many different arguments to prove immortality. Many of the proofs, however, come far short of really proving it. Plato, for example, tied his belief in the immortality of the soul to a belief that the soul had always existed from all eternity, but that would make the individual soul on a par with God Himself. Perhaps the strongest philosophical argument for immortality is the moral and ethical one. Nearly all intelligent philosophers believe that there is a moral order in the universe, and that right is rewarded and evil punished. But when we try to make that system work in this life we find that there are far too many exceptions to it to make it of any real value. Judged by any fair standards, the good persons do not always prosper in proportion to their goodness; nor do the evil suffer for their sins. If this life is all, then that belief in a moral universe, to say nothing of a belief in a fair, holy God, must be relegated to the scrap pile. There must be a life beyond the grave in which the accounts of this life can be squared.

We may recognize some force also in the universality of the belief in immortality. There must be something in it for so many persons in so many different places and ages to believe that it is true. We find men from the earliest times burying the bodies of their loved ones carefully, placing food and other provisions for further life, giving instructions for the journey to the other world, and so on. Maybe it was only wishful thinking, but somehow they were convinced that death was not the end.

Some of these reasons carry more weight than others, but no one of them is quite conclusive. We long for someone who has died to come forth and prove that the grave is not the end. And we do have just that kind of conclusive proof. Jesus of Nazareth was put to death and laid away in a tomb. On the third day that tomb was empty, and Jesus Himself began to appear to those disciples who knew Him best. He appeared many times over a period of forty days. Then He ascended into heaven.

It is amazing how strong the proof for the resurrection of

Jesus can be made even for those who do not believe in the inspiration of Scripture. We have extremely early evidence for this belief. Just see the long list of witnesses in I Corinthians 15, written less than thirty years after the event took place, when many of the witnesses were still alive. None of the various accounts of the Gospels can be placed much later. These documents were produced by honorable men, by men who were in a position to know the truth, by men who believed the truth so firmly that they gave their whole lives to the propagation of it. The Resurrection changed the tragedy of Calvary to the triumph of the empty tomb and Pentecost. It was made central in the preaching of the earliest Christian evangelists. It cannot be explained as the product of wishful thinking, because all the documents agree in telling that the disciples were not expecting Jesus to rise and demanded strong proof before they came to believe that He had risen. Apart from all theories of inspiration, impartial historians recognize that the resurrection of Jesus from the dead is one of the best attested facts of ancient history.

Those of us who believe that the Bible is God's inspired revelation have all of these things and more. The Old Testament makes a beginning of the revelation, but when we come to the New Testament the message is full and certain. The teachings of Jesus and Paul and all the other writers are in complete agreement. The fact of immortality is clearly stated over and over again. That fact is used to comfort those who have lost their loved ones. It is used to inspire men to live the Christian life no matter what the opposition may be. We are urged to remember that we are but strangers and sojourners down here, that our citizenship is in heaven. We are told to lay up our treasures in heaven rather than on earth. No one who has the New Testament and believes in it as a part of God's Word need be in the slightest doubt. "Death is swallowed up in victory. O death, where is thy sting? O grave, where is thy victory?"

The thing that we call death does bring these physical bodies of ours to an end in their present form. The really important part of us, our soul, that which makes us unique personalities, lives on. Death is just a door into another life; it is not the end.

CHAPTER THREE

TWO PLACES TO SPEND ETERNITY

THE grave is not the end. Our bodies are to be laid into the grave, but our souls live on throughout eternity. How much can we know about that eternal existence? Naturally, there is much that we do not know and cannot hope to know until we come to experience it for ourselves. Yet God has seen fit to allow us to know something. Especially, He has told us enough about the eternal life to allow us to make the proper preparation for it. It cannot be emphasized too much that this brief span of life here on this earth is not what God created us for primarily. Now we are, as it were, in a school preparing for life; when we leave this brief existence, we shall be graduating into real life. This Scriptural view does not rob this life of its real value; nor should it make us despise or neglect the challenges and joys of the present. The student who gets the most out of his college days is not the student who makes the college life an end in itself. Nor is it the student who refuses to enter into the work of the college and looks forward to the time when college will be over and he can then begin to enjoy life. It is the one who uses every opportunity to the full and who sees how those college opportunities are fitting him for the years that lie beyond graduation. Just so the Christian must be careful to keep the balance between this world and the next. We are in this life now, and we should get the most out of it; but we may do that best only if we live it in the light of the eternal life to follow.

Scripture teaches very plainly that there are two places where men will spend eternity. One very clear passage is found in the teachings of Jesus in Matthew 25:31-46, where we find the following words: "When the Son of man shall come in his glory . . . before him shall be gathered all nations: and he shall separate them one from another, as a shepherd divideth his sheep from the goats . . . Then shall the King say unto them on his right hand, Come, ye blessed of my Father, inherit the kingdom prepared for you from the foundation of the world . . . Then shall he say also unto them on the left hand, Depart from me, ye cursed, into everlasting fire, prepared for the devil and his angels . . . And these shall go away into everlasting punishment: but the righteous into life eternal." It is needless to give other passages, as anyone can find them in abundance throughout Scripture, especially throughout the New Testament.

There are some, however, who teach, in direct contradiction to the plain teachings of Scripture, that ultimately all human beings will be saved. They affirm that God is too good to allow anyone to go away into eternal punishment.

It is true that God is good, and all of us glory in that fact. The goodness of God led Him to provide a way by which every single man could be saved, but it did not force Him to compel every man to accept the way provided. "God so loved the world, that he gave his only begotten Son, that *whosoever* believeth in him should not perish, but have everlasting life." The love of God was so great that He gave His only Son to die to make it possible for the vilest sinner to be delivered from his sins. And God made the condition of acceptance a very simple one: belief in Jesus Christ. But God made us men, not machines; He gives us the right to make our own decisions.

Of course it is hard to think of anyone's suffering through all eternity, and no one has given an explanation that is entirely satisfactory. But it would be far harder to believe that God would treat all men alike in spite of the tremendous differences we actually see all about us. The Universalist takes an entirely too light view of sin. Sin deserves eternal punishment. If the saintliest mother and public enemy number one, if the believer and the unbeliever, are all going to be treated alike, what kind of God could we believe in then? Why should we have any religion at all? Why should anyone try to be good? What meaning would there be in life after all? Universalism raises far more questions than it answers.

There are some who believe that there will be other chances

after death. The nearest thing to a justification for that belief to be found in Scripture is the very difficult verse, I Peter 3:19, about Christ preaching "unto the spirits in prison." We cannot go into the many interpretations of that verse, but we can say that it would be far from safe to wait until after death to believe on Jesus on the basis of a barely possible interpretation of this most obscure verse. Scripture teaches very plainly that we have our chance to believe in this life. In the parable of Dives and Lazarus, Jesus tells us about the great gulf that is fixed. Dives could never hope to get where Lazarus was; his only thought was that his brothers should be warned so they would not come into the place where he was. Scripture says nothing about any doctrine of reincarnation such as is taught in some religions. Those who hold this theory say: "After you have lived this life well, you may come back in a somewhat higher state of existence, until, step by step, you may be absorbed into divinity; if not, you may be dropped a notch or two until you finally determine to live in the right direction." This is hardly a reasonable view of life; it is certainly not a Scriptural one.

The Roman Catholic Church makes a great deal of its doctrine of purgatory. That, it is to be noted, is not another chance to believe in Christ after this life. Purgatory is supposed to be a place where believers go at death to have their sins burned away before they enter heaven, especially the sins they committed after believing in Christ. It is believed that those still living may shorten the pains of purgatory by praying for the souls of their loved ones, or by having masses celebrated for them, or by doing works of supererogation for them, or by getting some of the saints to credit them with some of their works of supererogation.

No mention whatever is made of purgatory in Scripture. The most that anyone can claim is that a very few passages seem to imply it, such as the statement that there is no forgiveness for the sin against the Holy Spirit in this life or the next (Matthew 12:31, 32), or the famous passage of the keys and the binding on this earth and in heaven (Matthew 16:18, 19). If you start with a doctrine of purgatory, you can twist a few passages to fit in with it; but that is as far as you can go with Scripture. The

Catholic recognizes that his real proof for purgatory is not Scripture but tradition. The Catholic puts tradition on a par with, or even above, Scripture, a thing which the Protestant would never dream of doing. Certain passages of the early Church Fathers can be made to imply purgatory, though those passages do not become at all clear until we come to the time of Augustine in the fifth century. Gregory the Great, who died in 604, gave the doctrine its fullest statement, and it occupied a most prominent place throughout the Church until the Reformation, and still does in the Catholic Church.

The doctrine of purgatory dishonors the saving work of Christ. We believe that His salvation takes care of all our sins, not just part of them. We do not believe that anyone, even the most saintly, can do a work of supererogation—can be better than is necessary for himself. Nor do we believe that the celebration of a mass, nor the doing of penance, nor the saying of prayers, nor the burning of candles by anyone on this earth can have any effect on the souls of those who have passed on into the new life.

According to the plain teaching of Scripture there are two places where men are to spend eternity: heaven and hell. There are some things that we may know and know definitely about these two places, and there are some things that we cannot know as yet.

No one knows just the geography of heaven and hell. When the earth was considered as something like a flat table, it was assumed that heaven was above it and hell beneath it. Now, of course, we know that the earth is round, and the problem is somewhat complicated. But modern science has increased the size of the universe for us so much that there is plenty of room in it for God to have many heavens and hells. There are some intimations that possibly this earth itself will be a part of the eternal heaven when all the curse due to sin has been removed from it. Nothing certain can be said about where heaven and hell will be, but we can be sure that God knows of an abundance of satisfactory places.

Nor do we know exactly what kinds of bodies we shall have throughout eternity. Jesus answered the objection of the Sadducees by saying that things are going to be different in heaven;

there will be no marrying there, but we shall be like the angels. (Matthew 22:29, 30.) The great resurrection chapter of I Corinthians (chapter 15) tells us that our resurrection bodies will be very different from these mortal bodies of ours. We sow a little seed, and a great tree comes up. Our resurrection bodies will have something of that same relationship to our present bodies. There will be individuality and personality. We shall be able to recognize our loved ones and have fellowship with them. But in many respects our resurrection bodies will not be subject to the limitations of our human bodies, especially in respect to those limitations caused by sin. We have a hint as to the nature of our resurrection bodies in the body of Jesus after He came from the tomb; in many respects it was the same body, but there were significant differences. The spirit seems to have taken more complete control over the physical. But we cannot be sure that our bodies will be like His in every respect, especially when we remember that it was necessary for Him to appear to the disciples who still had their human, physical bodies.

What shall we be doing throughout eternity? Again we find that there are some things we know and some we do not.

We know that heaven will be a place of eternal happiness, while hell will be a place of eternal torment. We know that the joys of heaven will be far more wonderful than anything that we can now imagine, and the torments of hell far more terrible.

Scripture gives us some glorious pictures of heaven and some awful ones of hell. How much of those pictures is literal and how much figurative? No one should give a dogmatic answer to that question. The writers of Scripture had to use human language or we would not have been able to understand them. But human language is completely inadequate to describe the spiritual realities. Try to describe a magnificent sunset to a person who has always been blind, or a Beethoven symphony to one who has always been deaf; the nearest you can come to doing that is by likening the thing he has not experienced to something he has, and you still recognize that the description is far from adequate.

"Eye hath not seen, nor ear heard, neither have entered into the heart of man, the things which God hath prepared for them that love him," Paul (I Corinthians 2:9) quoted from Isaiah 64:4. Scripture gives us the most beautiful pictures of heaven. We may be sure that those pictures will be fulfilled literally or even more wonderfully. For those who are tired of the hard work on earth, there is rest in heaven; but surely no one would be satisfied simply to rest throughout eternity. For those who are sad, it is said that God Himself will wipe away their tears; though literally we need not believe that there will be any tears in heaven. For those who have suffered the hardships of poverty in this life, heaven is pictured as a place where the very streets are paved with gold. Those who love music will have the opportunity of singing with the heavenly choirs. All of us will join in the eternal chants of praise to God. Kipling catches the spirit of Scripture when he pictures heaven as a place where the artist can have real saints to draw from, and where only God will be his critic. Each one of us may paint his own picture of heaven and may make it just as wonderful as possible; and heaven will be all that and far more.

Hell is just the opposite. We do not know whether there will be actual fire and brimstone there or not. It is probable that spiritual bodies would not be affected by those things. But we do know that Scripture uses the most terrible words possible in its descriptions of hell.* Fire, burning sulphur, worms, the valley of Hinnom, weeping, wailing, and gnashing of teeth, many stripes—are any of these things very attractive to us? There may or may not be a literal lake of fire, but if it is not that it will be something far worse than that. Milton and Dante and others have taken the hints of Scripture and have expanded them, but the most terrible human picture can never do justice to the reality.

Some of the smaller cults and certain modern theologians teach that hell is not a place of eternal punishment but is simply the annihilation of the wicked. Certainly it would be easier for the sinner to look forward to capital punishment rather than life imprisonment in such a case, but that is not the teaching of Scripture. Nearly every description of hell in the Bible uses the words "ever-

---

*Such descriptions as Matthew 13:42; Mark 9:43, 44; Luke 12:47; Revelation 21:8; and many others.

[25]

lasting" or "eternal" or some equivalent. Then such a belief would directly contradict the faith in the immortality of the soul; no one of the arguments from Scripture or from reason would prove the immortality of only the believer's soul. Annihilation itself would be terrible enough for a soul that was made to live throughout eternity with God, but hell is even worse than that.

Thus there are those two places where men must spend eternity. We have the opportunity of making our choice in this life. Each one of us knows how that choice must be made. We shall quote only the one familiar verse, "For God so loved the world, that he gave his only begotten Son, that whosoever *believeth in him* should not perish, but have everlasting life."

There are only those two places, but when do men enter into them? Scripture does not give much chronological information about such matters, but there are certain indications that allow us to draw some rather clear inferences. We are told that in the last days of this age there will be a new heaven and a new earth. We are told that there will be a resurrection of our bodies. Evidently, at death the souls of believers go to be with God and enter into a period of bliss. Lazarus is spoken of as being in Abraham's bosom while Dives' brothers are still living. In Revelation the souls of the martyrs are pictured as being beneath the altar, asking God how long it would be before things were made right. This intermediate state of bliss goes into the final state when the Kingdom of God is established in all its fullness, when our resurrection bodies are united with our souls, and when we enter into the new heavens and the new earth.

Likewise Dives is pictured as being in torment, so it is probable that there is also a temporary abode for the wicked, to which they are sent at death, there to await the final resurrection and judgment.

CHAPTER FOUR

JESUS IS COMING AGAIN

THERE are some who call themselves Christians who believe that Jesus of Nazareth was only a man—a good man, a great teacher, a splendid example, but only a man. He died the death of a martyr. He did not rise from the dead. He will never come to earth again. This "radical" interpretation of Christianity directly contradicts the New Testament at many vital points, and has never been accepted as the true position of historic Christianity.

This is not the place to attempt to prove the deity of Jesus or those other related truths. We believe in the truth of the Biblical presentation. We accept the doctrine of the deity as well as the humanity of Jesus. We believe in Him as a great and good man, as a matchless teacher, as a perfect example. But we believe that His death was an atonement for the sins of the world, not merely a tragic martyrdom. We believe that He rose from the dead on the third day, and we believe that He is coming again. All of these things are integral parts of the common faith of historic Christianity.

The blessed hope of the second coming of our Lord is not the monopoly of any small group of Christians, as some mistakenly believe. Everyone who accepts the Bible as his rule of faith and practice—and that includes the vast majority of all Christians throughout all the ages—believes that Jesus is coming again. Conservative, Bible-believing Christians may differ about their theories of the millennium—they may be premillenarians, postmillenarians, or nonmillenarians—but they all unite in believing that Jesus is coming again.

The Old Testament predicted the coming of the Messiah in glory to establish the Kingdom of God, and all the Jews were longing for the fulfillment of those predictions. They did not recognize the fact that the Old Testament also predicted a coming of the

Messiah in humiliation and suffering, such as in the wonderful Suffering Servant passage in Isaiah 53. When Jesus came, the majority of the Jews refused to recognize Him as their Messiah. Even the disciples of Jesus found it very difficult to believe that Jesus would have to be rejected, to suffer, and to die. It is easier for us now, after the first coming, to see how that was necessary and to see how it fulfilled certain of those Old Testament predictions.

Jesus came the first time in humiliation, to make atonement for our sins. But those other predictions of the Old Testament are still to be fulfilled, about His coming in glory. And to the predictions of the Old Testament the New Testament adds many even more explicit ones. Let us quote only a few of them.

Jesus said, in Matthew 24: 27: "For as the lightning cometh out of the east, and shineth even unto the west; so shall also the coming of the Son of man be."

Just a bit further on, in Matthew 24: 30: "And they shall see the Son of man coming in the clouds of heaven with power and great glory."

He said, in John 14: 3: "And if I go and prepare a place for you, I will come again, and receive you unto myself; that where I am, there ye may be also."

The angels said to the disciples as Jesus was taken up from them, in Acts 1: 11: "Ye men of Galilee, why stand ye gazing up into heaven? this same Jesus, which is taken up from you into heaven, shall so come in like manner as ye have seen him go into heaven."

The Apostle Paul said, in I Thessalonians 4: 16: "For the Lord himself shall descend from heaven with a shout, with the voice of the archangel, and with the trump of God."

In Hebrews 9: 28 we read: "So Christ was once offered to bear the sins of many; and unto them that look for him shall he appear the second time without sin unto salvation."

At the beginning of the book of Revelation, 1: 7, we read: "Behold, he cometh with clouds; and every eye shall see him." The Second Coming is prominent throughout Revelation. Then the book comes to a close, 22: 20, with: "He which testifieth these things saith, Surely I come quickly. Amen. Even so, come, Lord Jesus."

These are only a few of the many passages that occur throughout Scripture. Surely there need be no doubt in the mind of any Bible-believing Christian. Jesus is coming again.

And all of the passages make it clear that Jesus is coming again in glory, in triumph. He is coming to reap the full fruits of His first coming and of all of the divine drama of redemption. The first time He came He wore a crown of thorns, but it will be a different kind of crown the next time. The first time He came to make possible a way by which sinful men could be saved from their sins. The second time He is coming to gather together all those who have accepted His offer of salvation. When He came the first time He rode upon a lowly ass. When He comes again He will be riding upon a white horse of triumphant victory. He came the first time to plant the tiny seed of the Kingdom of God, but at His Second Coming we shall see the seed grown up into a mighty tree, we shall see the fullness of the Kingdom.

All of us believe that Jesus is coming again to separate mankind into the two classes, the saved and the unsaved. "When the Son of man shall come in his glory . . . he shall set the sheep on his right hand, but the goats on the left." (Matthew 25: 31, 33.) Some Christians believe that there will be one final judgment, while others believe that the judgment will take place in several phases. All agree, however, that the separation will be intimately connected with the coming again of our Lord.

Some Christians believe that the Second Coming will be followed immediately by a period of temporary, Utopian bliss on earth before the final glory of eternal heaven, while others believe that He will take His saints immediately to their eternal home. But all agree that His Second Coming will bring this present age to an end and will introduce an age infinitely better, and that heaven will come, either immediately or after some thousand years.

Where will Jesus come when He comes again? Some believe that it will be to the literal city of Jerusalem, while others are not so sure of that. The important thing for us to remember is that His coming will be like the lightning, shining from the east to the west. He will not come to an obscure corner of the earth to be seen of only a select few. No, every eye shall see Him. We shall not need to make pilgrimages to the Holy City or climb to the mountain-tops, for when He comes, wherever we may be, we shall see him.

Some are frightened when they think about the Second Coming. No Christian should be. Every non-Christian ought to be. The Christian should look forward to the coming of Jesus as to the coming back of his very best friend who has been absent on a long journey. The Christian should recognize the Second Coming as the final defeat of the power of Satan and the triumph of the cause of Christ. The Christian should look forward to standing in the presence of his Master and hearing those blessed words, "Well done, good and faithful servant; enter thou into the joy of thy Lord."

There are some minor points in connection with the Second Coming about which Christians are not able to see eye to eye, but we should recognize clearly that we all agree on the things of real importance. These minor differences should never be allowed to obscure the blessed hope of the Second Coming of our Lord and Master, Jesus Christ, or to disrupt the fellowship of Christians.

CHAPTER FIVE

THE BOOK OF REVELATION

No BOOK in the whole Bible has been the subject of more controversy than the book of Revelation. Manifestly it would be impossible to make a full presentation of all those matters in a brief treatment like the present volume—even if the author himself had the solution to all the problems. But there may be value in going over some of the major points, in seeing some of the divergent theories that are held, and in recognizing how much real agreement there is among all Bible scholars as to the important messages of the book. No student of the future can go very far without meeting this great book.

The book was written by a Christian prophet named John. Early tradition identifies that John with the Apostle John, and most conservative scholars believe that that identification is correct. We may recognize, however, that the question of authorship has no major bearing upon the message of the book.

It is generally agreed that the book was written during the latter part of the reign of the Roman emperor Domitian, who reigned from 81 to 96 A. D. It was written from the Island of Patmos, in the Aegean Sea, to the churches of Ephesus and the surrounding cities. Seven churches are specifically named in the seven letters in chapters 2 and 3, each church being in a city that can easily be located on the map.

The historical background of the book is also clear. For a long time it had been customary to elevate Roman emperors to the rank of deity upon death. The emperor Domitian, however, decided to claim the title of god during his lifetime. That was a somewhat different matter. A dead emperor could not force people to worship him, and the live emperors did not exert themselves to compel their subjects to worship their dead and deified predecessors. But Domitian claimed deity while he was still alive, and while he was still able to enforce his claims. Some sections of the Empire seem to have taken the claims more seriously than others. The officials of the Roman province of Asia, with Ephesus as its capital, were determined to make their subjects bow down before the image of the living emperor. Most of the Roman citizens had many gods already, so it was a simple matter to add just one more. The Christians, however, believed in worshipping only the one Triune God. To worship Domitian would be to deny their God. So the Christians were determined not to give in to the demands of Rome, and the Roman officials were just as determined that the Christians must bow down to Domitian. To force their demands they made use of all kinds of persecutions. John himself was sent to the prison island of Patmos. Some of the leaders of the churches were martyred. The Christians were boycotted; only those who could produce evidence that they had worshipped the image of the Emperor could carry on their normal trade in the markets; others had to face starvation. Jesus had told His disciples to do their duty to Caesar and to God. Now the demands of God and those of Caesar are diametrically opposed, and it becomes imperative that the Christians must choose whether they will obey God or man. We can get some idea of the position of those early Christians when we see the demands made by the totalitarian states of Germany and Japan upon their Christian citizens. Some of the weaker members of the churches could not stand the pressure, so they fell away. John saw that it was a time of the greatest crisis for the Church. The Christians must be made to see the importance of the issues involved and must be inspired to remain true to God in spite of all the terrible persecutions that the powerful empire could devise. The book of Revelation, under the inspiration of the Holy Spirit, was John's contribution to that end.

But John was faced with a difficult problem. How could he get his message to the Christians when he himself was in a Roman prison island and all the Christians were carefully watched by the Romans? To speak openly against Rome would only make matters worse for himself and for any who might possess a copy of such a book. If John could ever hope to get his message to the other Christians, he would have to couch it in such language that it would be intelligible to the Christians but not to the Romans; and that is just what he did. That explains why there is so much symbolism and figurative language of all kinds in the book. We may be sure that John used symbols that his readers could understand. Some of those symbols we can very easily understand today; some of them can be understood only in part. We may make several intelligent guesses about some of them; and some are complete mysteries to us even now. When we have national elections we see donkeys and elephants in nearly every newspaper, and there are words placed in their mouths. College football teams are represented by bulldogs, yellow jackets, mules, and goats, fighting with one another and speaking various uncomplimentary words. We know exactly what is meant by these cartoons, though someone living many years in the future might draw strange conclusions from them.

So if you take everything in the book of Revelation literally you will make it a book of fantastic ideas, but when you get into the spirit of the symbols that are used you can see it for the inspired and inspiring book of genius that it is.

Let us look briefly at some of the theories of interpretation of the book as a whole. Various names are used for them, but we shall employ the ones in most common use. And we shall limit ourselves to the most important theories.

First we may mention the continuous-historical theory. That theory makes the book of Revelation a kind of almanac. Those who hold to this theory believe that God wrote the history of the world into the book of Revelation. Some of these students start the history at the beginning of the world, while others of them start it at some time in the early Christian era. Then from whatever beginning they take, they work on down through the book until they come to their own time, and they always consider their own time right at the end of this era. They identify the different paragraphs and chapters of Revelation with the outstanding events in history. The identifications are, of course, very fanciful. As time goes on and the end of time does not come, these students must stretch their scheme out like an accordion and must change their identifications all down the line. Anyone who studies this kind of interpretation over a period of time can see easily that the whole thing is pure guesswork and will make the book a Chinese puzzle. These students are able to show considerable ingenuity at times, but practically all Bible scholars are agreed that their theory is far from the truth.

Next let us look at the futurist interpretation of the book. Most futurist scholars start their futurist interpretation at chapter 4, after the letters to the seven churches. Then they consider all of the rest of the book a description of the events of the last days, of the events immediately preceding the Second Coming and on down into eternity. Some of them may be barely beginning in our own time, though most of them are still in the future; for the first readers of the book they were all in the far distant future. Some of the futurists take the book literally, while others recognize the use of figurative language. Nearly all scholars recognize that the Revelation contains some predictions of the last times, but most of them believe that the complete futurist position is not the best. The complete futurist position loses sight of the historical situation of those early Asia Minor churches and looks over symbols that seem clearly to apply directly to first-century conditions. John pointed the eyes of his readers to the final victory of Christ, but he did not tell them to hide their heads in the sand, like the traditional ostrich, and fail to see the tragic affairs of their own time. The complete futurist interpretation cannot be so easily shown to be untrue, because its identifications are all with events which the futurists believe are yet to be.

The preterist theory of interpretation emphasizes the historical background of the churches of Asia Minor in the latter part of the first century. It interprets the symbols in a way to make them give an interpretation of the mighty events that were transpiring at that very time. In this light the book becomes a message of real encouragement and inspiration to its original readers, and its messages may be appropriated by all its readers in so far as their conditions are like those of its first ones. Some of the preterists consider the book a purely human product, thinking that when the author describes the events of the far future, he is giving simply his own human guess about it. Other preterists treat the book as a truly inspired book, believing that when it deals with the last things, it is a divine revelation about them rather than a human guess.

Some earnest, intelligent Bible scholars will continue to prefer the futurist position. Others will prefer the preterist. Many will see elements of truth in both the futurist and the preterist, and that is the position that seems most plausible to this author. Surely the Apostle John must have had the situation of himself and his friends clearly in mind as he wrote. Many of the symbols seem definitely to apply to the Roman Empire and to the Christian Church of the first century. But from time to time the author tells his readers to turn their eyes down into the future and see the cause of Christ triumphing completely over all the forces of evil.

Nearly all students of the book, except those who hold to the continuous-historical theory, believe that there are synchronizations in the book. The book does not start at some certain time and then move down in chronological order until it comes to the end. It will start and work down to the end; then it will start over again. Some would say that there are only two of the synchronizations; others would say seven; others would prefer not to be dogmatic about the exact number. We ought to be careful about putting too much human chronology into prophecy. Remember that the Old Testament never gave the slightest indication that there would be more than nineteen hundred years between the first and the second comings of our Lord.

We cannot, of course, go into the details of an interpretation of the whole book, but we shall present the following brief outline of its contents, taken from the author's *A Conservative Introduction to the New Testament:* *

"I. SEVEN LETTERS, 1:1—3:22. After a short introduction, John gives a magnificent vision of the glorified Christ. The persecuted Christians of Asia Minor are reminded of the glories of their Lord, Who is far more glorious than even the Roman Em-

---

*Zondervan, 3rd ed., 1941, pp. 209-212. Quoted by permission.

peror. Remember that He is with you, no matter who may be against you. This glorified Christ knows what is going on in the various churches, and He sends to each one a letter, telling the real condition of the church and warning of certain dangers, commending certain good features, telling the punishment that is in store for those who fail and the glorious rewards that are in store for those who remain true. Prepare for persecution by looking up to the glorified Christ, and by looking within, to weed out the bad and strengthen the good.

"II. SEVEN SEALS, 4:1—8:1. As an introduction to this section, John presents a vision of God on His throne. He lives; He rules; all that happens, happens in accordance with His will. Then the Lamb takes a roll of destiny and opens, one by one, its seven seals. The first four seals bring forth four riders on colored horses, representing, probably, triumphant militarism, bloodshed, famine, and death. Those Asian Christians knew well that that was a correct picture of the conditions under which they were living under Rome. With little adaptation, that is a picture of the conditions under which Christians are still living. At the opening of the fifth seal, the scene changes to heaven, and we see beneath the altar the souls of those who had died for their faith. They are still interested in the conditions on earth, and they ask God how long He is going to allow the good to suffer and the evil to triumph. They are told that the present condition must last some time longer until all the elect have been gathered in; in God's own good time things will be made right. At the sixth seal, we are taken down into the last days and see the calamities that are to accompany the end of the world and the punishment that God is going to send upon the ungodly. Then there is a little interlude in which we see that God is going to protect those that are His from all the calamities, and we see a little foretaste of the glories that will be theirs. The seventh seal brings a half-hour's silence, allowing the reader to imagine the glories of eternity, or serving as an introduction to the next great action.

"III. SEVEN TRUMPETS, 8:2—11:19. After a short introduction, seven trumpeters sound their trumpets, one by one. The trumpets go more into detail in working out the punishment that God is sending and will send upon the ungodly world. The first four trumpets give terrible pictures of the wrath of God as it affects nature, the earth, the sea, the rivers, and the heavenly bodies. The fifth and sixth give vivid pictures of the punishment sent on men themselves. Then again we have an interlude, giving several short visions, emphasizing again the fact that God will preserve those who are His. The seventh trumpet brings in the establishment of the eternal kingdom of God.

"IV. MISCELLANEOUS VISIONS, 12:1—14:20. The woman, probably the Church, bears a manchild, Christ. The Dragon, Satan, is waiting to kill Him at His birth. He is taken up into heaven. Satan goes up to try to kill Him there. Satan is thrown out of heaven to the earth. Satan then tries to destroy the woman, the Church. Again he is unsuccessful. To the aid of the Dragon come two Beasts, probably representing the Roman Empire and the Roman Religion, especially emperor worship. So the anti-Christian trinity is completed.

"But we see other pictures. A great host of the elect is on Mount Zion. These and the angels sing their songs of praise to God.

"Then again we go down to the end of the world and see it pictured under the common figure of a harvest.

"V. SEVEN BOWLS, 15:1—16:21. After an introduction, seven angels pour out the contents of their seven bowls, one by one. The bowls have similarities with the trumpets and with the Egyptian plagues. They present more terrible pictures of the wrath of God against the ungodly world, leading up again to the end of the world and the final conflict between good and evil.

"VI. MISCELLANEOUS VISIONS, 17:1—22:21. The fall of the mighty city of Babylon is described in the most vivid detail. Rome, and all wicked cities like Rome and old Babylon, will receive their just dues.

"The Royal Warrior, Christ, comes and overthrows the two Beasts and consigns them to eternal torment. Rome and her religion—wicked states and false religions of all time—receive their rewards.

"Satan himself is overcome by Christ and sent finally to hell.

"The book reaches its glorious climax with a wonderful word picture of heaven. Those who are faithful to Christ may incur persecution on earth, but they will enjoy eternal bliss in heaven. But the ungodly will have no part in heaven.

"Then there is a concluding section, warning against making any changes in the book, urging Christians to remain faithful, and praying for the coming again of our Lord."

There are many of the details of the book that will continue to be of uncertain interpretation because we cannot hope to reconstruct the historical conditions of those early Christians with completeness. But the book certainly rewards the diligent student. In the midst of differences of interpretation about the details, we ought all to recognize the many clear and unmistakable messages of the book, messages that the world sorely needs at all times, but especially at those times when it is so difficult to be a real Christian. God is reigning over the world—not Domitian, or Napoleon, or the Kaiser, or Mussolini, or Hitler, or anyone else. God knows what is going on here on earth, what His children are suffering for Him. The book of destiny is in the hands of God and His Messiah. It is hard to be a Christian, but it is more than worth any sacrifice. The cause of Christ can never be destroyed, no matter how powerful its enemies may become. Sin will be punished and virtue rewarded. In God's own good time the Kingdom of God will be established by the final overthrow of Satan and the complete victory of Christ.

CHAPTER SIX

THEORIES OF THE MILLENNIUM

~~~~~~

WE COME now to a subject on which hundreds of volumes have been written. It will not be our purpose to go into all of the intricacies of the theories but to see at least the main points involved in each one.

It should be recognized clearly that we are coming into the realm of the theoretical at this point. Earnest, devoted, Bible-believing Christians are still differing among themselves in their interpretation of the Biblical teaching about the millennium. It is simply not fair when a person holding any one of the theories claims that his group alone is faithful to the teachings of the Bible.

Nor should the proponents of any one theory classify as ignoramuses or fanatics those who hold to another theory. The fact is that all of the millenarian groups have had some ignorant and fanatical members—and also some very sane and intelligent ones.

The members of one school have often claimed that all the outstanding Bible students are on their side; another school has claimed nearly all of the professors in the theological seminaries. The problem is not to be solved by counting noses. Unfortunately there is a tendency to recognize a man as a scholar if he agrees with your own position and to discredit him if he differs. The fact is that some of the finest scholars may be found holding each one of the millenarian theories.

Some Christians have made one particular theory a test of orthodoxy and have elevated their own theory to the position of a fundamental of the faith. That is most unfortunate. The belief in the Second Coming of our Lord may very definitely be considered a fundamental matter, but all those who hold to any one of the three millenarian theories believe firmly in that. The theories of the millennium are matters of interest and of some minor importance, but they should never be placed on a par with those great tenets of our faith which are really fundamental.

It is also most unfortunate that there has been so much heat, and at times so little light, in the millennial debates. Christians should love one another. It is perfectly proper to have friendly debates over such matters, but bitterness should always be avoided.

It is surprising how many Christians know of only two theories of the millennium and believe that you must be either a premillenarian or a postmillenarian. Actually there are three distinct theories, those two and the nonmillenarian. That latter view is actually one of the two ancient theories, going back, along with the premillenarian theory, to the writings of the earliest of the Apostolic Fathers. It is the postmillenarian theory that is really the modern one, having been first proposed by Daniel Whitby, who died in 1726. Before the time of Whitby the division was between millenarians, or chiliasts, and the nonmillenarians, or those who were not chiliasts. Whitby's postmillenarianism made it necessary for the millenarians to change their name to premillenarians.

Then it is also true that all too many Christians know only one of the theories, and probably know that one none too well.

Let us look, now, at each of the three theories.

PREMILLENARIANISM

The name of this theory comes from three Latin words meaning "before the thousand years." The name is used to indicate the belief that the Second Coming of our Lord is to take place before a period of a thousand years of universal peace and righteousness on earth.

The basic outline of the theory is as follows. The present age in which we are now living will be brought to an end with the Second Coming, which may take place at any time. When the Lord comes, He will institute His millennial reign on earth. When the millennium is over, there will be eternity, with heaven for the saved and hell for the unsaved.

What is the millennium itself, according to this theory? It is described primarily in Revelation 20: 1-6, though most premillenarians believe that there are many other passages in Scripture that should be considered descriptions of the millennium. All the scholars of this school believe that Christ will be reigning during this period and that Satan will be in the bottomless pit until the end of the period. Righteousness will cover the earth. There may be some sin, but it will be kept in check by the power of Christ. All of them agree that there will be this period of Utopian bliss which will last for a thousand years, more or less literally.

Beyond that, regarding the millennium there is much about which premillenarians differ among themselves. Some believe that Christ will set up the throne of David again in Jerusalem and rule as an earthly king; others are not so sure. Some believe that those who have died in Christ will be raised when He comes and will reign with Him during the millennium on earth; others believe that their reign will be from above. There are the questions as to how those who have risen from the dead will mingle with those who have never died, as to whether persons will be born and die during the millennium, and other such problems. Some students claim to have an answer for every question, while others, probably more wisely, refrain from much dogmatism; they believe in the period of universal righteousness under the reign of Christ, but they do not care to state specifically the details of it.

The simple outline of the premillenarian theory can be found in Scripture by taking Revelation 19, 20, and 21 in chronological order. Chapter 19 tells about the Second Coming; chapter 20 has the millennium; and chapter 21 brings us to a description of heaven. Those who hold to the other theories call attention to the fact that there are synchronizations in Revelation, so it is by no means necessary to believe that those chapters must follow along in chronological order.

Many premillenarians believe in an outline of the last things that is quite a bit more detailed than the simple outline given above. As the outline becomes more complicated, there is more room for differences of opinion. No one of the fuller outlines can be found in any one place in Scripture; each must be made by putting together various passages found throughout Scripture. Let us look a bit at one of the typical fuller outlines.

The age in which we are living will be brought to an end by the Second Coming, but that Second Coming will take place in two phases, in the rapture and in the revelation. At the rapture phase, the dead in Christ will be raised and the living believers will be caught up from the earth, and together they will meet the Lord in the air. This first phase will not be known to the world at large; the ungodly will simply find that the Christians are mysteriously missing. Some believe that some Christians will not share in the rapture—namely, those who, like the foolish virgins, were not ready for the coming of their Lord. While some or all of the Christians are in the air with the Lord, there comes a period of Great Tribulation on earth. Most of these scholars identify this period as the last half of the seventieth week of Daniel, and think that it will last for three and a half years; some make it the whole of the seventieth week, or seven years; others do not care to dogmatize about the exact length. At the end of the Great Tribulation, there comes the revelation, and Christ and His saints come to earth, and Christ leads His forces to victory over the forces of Satan in the battle of Armageddon. Then there is a resurrection of the saints who died during the Great Tribulation. Then comes the millennium. At the end of that, Satan is loosed from the pit and makes one final effort to overthrow Christ. But Christ, in the battle of Gog and Magog, wins a complete victory. Then there is the final resurrection of the wicked dead and the judgment of the Great White Throne. Satan and his hosts are sent to an eternal hell, while God and His chosen ones enter the eternal bliss of heaven.

Some of the premillenarians believe that Scripture gives very exact predictions of the events of the last days, especially in the books of Daniel and Revelation. Many of them have tried to predict the exact course of events of both of the world wars of the twentieth century. It is necessary, of course, to put a very fanciful interpretation upon Scripture to see any references to the Kaiser, Woodrow Wilson, Hitler, Mussolini, Stalin, Roosevelt, and other modern world figures, yet these students can convince themselves that they are there. But it is easy to see that their "prophecies" are nothing but fairly intelligent guesses imposed upon a purely fanciful interpretation of Scripture. And the guesses must be continually overhauled as events prove them wrong. For example, a book written early in the second world war made much of Mussolini, saying that Scripture predicted that he would take the leadership in the Axis and set up the great world-wide Roman Empire; it also made much of the alliance between Germany and Russia. Very soon after the book was published, Russia came into the war on the side of the United Nations, and Mussolini and Italy began to take less and less part on the side of the Axis. Sane premillenarians would do well to avoid any such "light from prophecy" as that.

POSTMILLENARIANISM

The postmillenarians likewise believe in a millennium on earth, but they believe that the Second Coming will come *after* the thousand years (the Latin "post" means "after").

Some of the postmillenarians have just about as detailed a picture of the millennium as any premillenarian, though most of them do not care to be so certain. On the whole, they take the prophecies that they apply to the millennium somewhat less literally than most of the premillenarians.

These scholars believe that the Church will continue to spread the teachings and the spirit of Jesus until finally they will take control of the whole world. Then will come the reign of universal righteousness to last for a thousand years, or some long period. At the end of the millennium, Christ will come again. There will be the final resurrection of all the dead and the translation of all the living. There will be the final judgment, followed by eternity with its heaven and hell.

This is a brief description of the essentials of this theory. Some of those who hold to it go into more detail in outlining the world conditions that they believe will prevail during the period of the millennium, but as their descriptions become more detailed they differ more and more with each other. Some are quite sure that some form of socialism will be practiced, while others are quite as certain that it will be a slightly reformed capitalism. They all agree, however, that the principles of love and brotherhood as taught by Jesus Christ will be predominant.

It should be recognized that there are some scholars who call themselves postmillenarians but who hold to the distinctive non-millenarian views. It is much better to recognize the three different theories.

NONMILLENARIANISM

This theory has an unfortunate name. It implies that its holders do not believe in a part of Scripture, that they are somewhat liberal or radical. But such is not the case at all. Those who hold to this view believe in the twentieth chapter of Revelation just as strongly as anyone else; they simply do not believe in the *kind* of millennium that the premillenarians and the postmillenarians believe in. Some seek to hide the implication of the word by using the hybrid term amillenarianism, because the Greek negative "a" is not so well known as the Latin "non." The name may not be so good, but the theory is an ancient one, the one taught or implied in practically all of the creeds of Christendom, and the one that is held by probably the vast majority of Christians today who hold to any theory at all.

The outline of this theory is very simple. This present age will be brought to an end by the Second Coming of Christ, which may take place at any time. When Christ comes, there will be the final resurrection and translation of the living, the final judgment, and the eternal heaven and hell. That simple outline may be found over and over again in Scripture.

But where is the millenium? What is done with Revelation 20 and the other passages that deal with the millennium? Some of those passages are made to apply to heaven itself, while others are thought to apply to at least certain features of the present age. Specifically, Revelation 20 is made to apply primarily to the reign of the dead in Christ with Christ in the intermediate state, between the first coming of Christ and His Second Advent.

That period has already extended to more than nineteen hundred years instead of a thousand years, but it should be recognized that it is by no means necessary to take the numbers of the book of Revelation literally. But can Satan be said to be bound during this age? There is certainly much evidence of sin all about us. He is bound, though, in reference to those who have died in Christ, for he can no longer touch a single one of them. He may even be said to be bound on earth in the sense that Christ has made atonement for sin, and Satan's death warrant has been signed. Christ, as His disciples spread the Gospel, said that He saw Satan fall like lightning from heaven, which may have some connection with the binding of Revelation 20. Thus the nonmillenarians believe that the millennium of Revelation 20 is now in progress. Most of them believe that it applies primarily to the state of the blessed dead who are now reigning with Christ, though many believe that it may apply secondarily to the progress of the cause of Christ on earth.

There is pictured a great outbreak of evil before the coming of Christ. That does not mean, necessarily, that the earth will have to become any worse than it is now. The evil will continue to grow more evil and the good more good until Christ comes and ushers in the final victory for His cause of righteousness.

SOME EVALUATIONS OF THE THEORIES

Again let us emphasize the fact that all three theories are attempts by honest, Bible-believing Christians to interpret the teachings of Scripture itself. No one theory has a right to monopolize the word Scriptural for itself. Each student should seek to choose that theory which seems to harmonize most completely with the best interpretations of Scripture that he can find. He should understand all three theories, and if he decides to hold to one of the theories, he should have complete good will toward other Christians who may differ with him.

The premillenarian theory is able to interpret more Scripture literally than either of the other two theories. For some, that is a great advantage. It is probably the deciding factor for many.

But all intelligent students of Scripture realize that much figurative language is used in Scripture as in nearly all literature. A beautiful figure of speech in Shakespeare may be far more valuable than a simple prose statement in the morning newspaper. There is no real reason why a literal interpretation is to be preferred over a reasonable figurative interpretation. That is especially true in dealing with a book like Revelation, where the main millenarian passage occurs.

The premillenarians have been accused of being pessimists, and many of them seem to be. The more evil they can see in the world, the nearer they think the Second Coming is. That may well be true of the nonmillenarian as well. But it need not be true of either.

Some premillenarians are so sure that the end is at hand that they are not carrying on their present tasks in the proper way. We shall discuss this point later. Here let us state that we should all be ready for Christ whenever He may come, but that does not mean that we should stop our work and wait in white robes for Him to appear.

The postmillenarian theory emphasizes the importance of the Christian's work in spreading the Gospel and the Christian way of life. Those who hold to either of the other views should catch this emphasis and make use of it themselves in connection with their own theory. All of us ought to be doing our very best to lead men to believe in Christ as their Saviour and to make His teachings the standard of our living, to make the will of God done in earth as it is in heaven just as far as it is in our power to do so. That is our task. God can bring our work to an end whenever He sees fit to send His Son to bring this age to its consummation.

The great disadvantage of the postmillenarian theory is that it gives a negative date to the Second Coming. Certainly the age of universal peace and righteousness is not here yet, and if that must come and must last a thousand years or so, no one of us can hope to be alive when our Lord comes again at its end. A belief in the possibly imminent Second Coming fades away.

The postmillenarian theory was very popular in the early days of the evolutionary theory. It became popular to believe that everything was getting better and better. Soon the Golden Age would be brought in by man's own efforts. We are coming to realize that that superficial optimism was hardly justified; as yet, at least, man is still very much under the control of the power of sin. This theory was the latest to arise, and it seems to be on the verge of dying a natural death. Very few real postmillenarians can be found. Some continue to use the name, but they define their theory in such a way as to make it really the nonmillenarian theory.

The nonmillenarian theory has the virtue of being very simple and of being found repeatedly in Scripture. It takes many passages figuratively, and for that reason some cannot follow it.

Probably the most difficult problem that the nonmillenarian must face is the problem of the restoration of the Jews. There are passages in Scripture that seem to indicate that there will be a mass turning of the Jews to Christ. The premillenarian can believe that that will occur during the Great Tribulation or the millennium, while the postmillenarian has plenty of time before the end. The nonmillenarian has no time after the Second Coming for such a mass conversion. If such a conversion is to take place, he must believe that it will take place before the Second Coming. Then the Second Coming cannot be imminent, because the conversion has not yet taken place. That is a real difficulty, but not necessarily an insuperable one. It may be that there will be such a mass conversion before the Second Coming, but, on the other hand, Scripture has much to say about a spiritual Israel as well as a literal Israel. And it is possible to interpret Scripture so as to believe that God has finished with the literal Israel and is now dealing exclusively with the spiritual Israel, the descendants by faith from the faithful father Abraham. Most nonmillenarians believe that our Lord may come at any time, though they would prefer to be uncertain as to exactly how God will deal with Israel.

Thus we have surveyed some of the most important factors in this very complicated matter. Some readers may wish to go more deeply into the questions involved; if so, they will find an abundant literature on the subject in the systematic theologies and the many books on eschatology, the doctrine of the last things. Unfortunately, nearly every author feels called upon to defend one theory and condemn all the others, so the student should read several works from men holding different theories.

In conclusion, let us again emphasize the fact that all Bible-believing Christians unite on the really important points of eschatology, and that the things about which we are still differing are at best minor matters.

Note: Those who wish to go into more detail as to the theories of the millennium will find an abundant literature available, though unfortunately most of it is rather technical and polemic. The three following books will probably give as good a presentation as any others: Premillenarian, *Jesus Is Coming,* by W. E. B. (W. E. Blackstone); Postmillenarian, *The Coming of the Lord,* by James H. Snowden; and Nonmillenarian, *The Basis of Millennial Faith,* by Floyd Hamilton. All of the systematic theologies will give a treatment of the subject, and brief treatments may be found in the articles on the millennium and eschatology in the Bible dictionaries and encyclopedias.

CHAPTER SEVEN

WHEN WILL THE END COME?

~~~~~~

MEN have been asking that question through the centuries. The disciples long ago said to Jesus, "Tell us, when shall these things be?" The sum of Jesus' answer was, "But of that day and that hour knoweth no man, no, not the angels which are in heaven, neither the Son, but the Father." (Mark 13: 4, 32.) Jesus said also, "For in such an hour as ye think not the Son of man cometh." (Matthew 24: 44.) These verses, and others that could be quoted, ought to make it perfectly clear that no human being can hope to know when Jesus is coming again. That is one of the mysteries that the Father has seen fit to keep for Himself; even Jesus Himself when He was on earth had to say that He did not know.

Yet down through the ages men have sought to be wiser than Scripture, wiser even than Jesus Himself. They have sought by various ways to discover what God says cannot be discovered. And from the earliest times men have been setting dates for the Second Coming. Some have been so unwise as to set the exact year, month, and day. Others go only so far as to say that the signs of the times prove conclusively that Jesus must come in the very near future.

One of the earliest Epistles of the New Testament was called forth by such a situation. Some of the members of the church at Thessalonica in some way had become assured that the Second Coming was at hand. They concluded, then, that there was no use going on with their regular work. "Why plant a crop? Jesus will be back before we can harvest it. Why work to save money? Jesus will return before we will have a chance of spending it." Paul saw clearly the danger of such an attitude, so to meet the situation he wrote the letter which we know as II Thessalonians. He reasons with those persons and shows them the fallacy of taking any such position. Then he tells the rest of the members of the church a very practical way of dealing with them if they will not listen to reason: "If any would not work, neither should he eat." (II Thessalonians 3: 10.) We may be sure that that policy brought those foolish persons to their senses.

It may be interesting to look briefly at some of the dates that have been set and the ways men have figured them out.

Irenaeus said that a day with the Lord was a thousand years. There were six days of creation followed by a day of rest. Therefore the world would last six thousand years; then there would be the thousand years of rest. If he is right, we have only to discover the year in which the world was created and add six thousand to it.

Tyconius said that the Second Coming would take place three and a half days (the last half of the seventieth week of Daniel) after the Crucifixion. That would mean 350 years after the year 30, or the year 380 A. D.

Many persons thought that Christ would come again a thousand years after He came the first time, so there was tremendous excitement as the year 1000 approached. When that passed, they thought that maybe the 1000 years should have been started with the Crucifixion, so they grew excited again when 1030 drew near. (Of course we know that Jesus was not born in the year 1 A. D., and we are not so sure of the year 30 for the year of the Crucifixion; but these scholars (?) were.)

Joachim in the year 1195 said that Jesus would come back about 1260. Whiston fixed the date at 1715. When that year passed, he admitted that he was wrong and fixed another date, 1734. When that date came and went, he was wise enough to choose one far enough in the future so that he would not have to admit another error during his lifetime, so he chose 1866. But that, too, has gone.

The author has heard of several exact dates being fixed in only recent years. For months there was an advertisement in the Atlanta papers that the end would come on June 3, 1941; when that day passed the advertisement stopped, but the Lord did not come again. After about a year's silence, the same person has started his advertisement again. Now he claims that the Second Coming will come within the next two and a half years. At least one of the books on the Great Pyramid says that the beginning of Christ's millennial rule will take place not later than September 17, 2001.

Thus men have been calculating the date from the earliest times. They have used various fanciful interpretations of Scripture, the signs of the Zodiac, astronomy, the architectural dimensions of the Great Pyramid, and all other kinds of supposed means of determining the date. No one who has seen something of the many failures in the past will be greatly moved by any of the modern guesses.

There is much more reason in the attempt of many to read the signs of the times to see reasons for believing that Jesus must come in the near future. Yet we find that men throughout the course of history have been convinced that their own time was at the very end of time.

Men have sought to identify the anti-Christ of Revelation with its number 666. The author has seen three "proofs" that Hitler is that number. During the first world war men were able to "prove" that it was the Kaiser. Tolstoi makes his hero prove that Napoleon fit the number. Peter Olivi found that the numerical value of Benedict written in Greek was 666, so he concluded that the pope of his day, Benedict XI, was the anti-Christ. During the Reformation it was popular for the Protestants to show how many of the Catholic leaders would fit the picture, and the Catholics returned the compliment by identifying the anti-Christ with Luther, Calvin, and the other reformers. Manifestly, John was using some cryptogram when he used the number 666, but he was certainly not thinking about a certain mediaeval pope or a modern dictator.

Another popular "sign of the times" has been the Jewish people. Every time Palestine comes to occupy a prominent place in the news, some "prophetic students" are assured that the end is at hand. Several times during World War I some men were certain that events were leading up to the battle of Armageddon, but they were wrong. Many are convinced that modern Zionism is a prelude to the events that will bring in the end, but Zionism continues to be a movement for only a tiny minority of the Jews. Nor is it certain that God must have a mass conversion of the literal Jews at any time.

Probably the most common "sign" has been the prevalence of evil. Scripture does indicate that there will be much evil in existence before the end. That evil may be headed up in a personal anti-Christ or Man of Sin, though that is by no means certain. Surely there is enough evil in the world today. Some say that there is so much evil that only the Second Coming can make it possible for existence to continue. We agree that there is much evil here, but any student of history can point out many eras in the past when men were just as certain that things had become so bad that the end must be at hand. That is especially true of times of great warfare. Many famous Bible students signed a manifesto during World War I in which they stated that the evil abroad in the world convinced them that the end was at hand. Much of the prophetic literature today emphasizes the prevalence of all kinds of sin. If the Lord should come today we could not tell Him that He had come too soon as there was not yet enough sin. But on the other hand we are not greatly impressed by the claims that He must come soon because the world is so much worse than it has ever been before.

It may be that before the Lord comes there may be certain signs that will be so clear that all observant Christians will recognize them. Now we may say that the signs seem purposely to be rather general ones.

We may conclude this discussion by repeating the verse with which we started: "But of that day and that hour knoweth no man, no, not the angels which are in heaven, neither the Son, but the Father." And we are not convinced that anyone is able to read the signs of the times definitely enough to prove that the time must be in the immediate future. God will send His Son back in His own good time. That time may be very near; it may be far in the future. Each one of us has the right to hope that that time may come in his own lifetime, to obtain all the courage and inspiration possible from the Blessed Hope. Yet each one should carry on the work God has given him to do as though the present age might last indefinitely.

How are we to be ready for the coming of that day? By stopping work, putting on our white robes, and sitting idly by until the end comes? By no means. To be ready for the coming of our Lord, each one of us should make perfectly sure that he is a believer in Christ; then he should seek to carry on his life in such a way that he would not be ashamed to have Jesus come and meet him at any time. There is no reason for hysteria or for a temporary *interim ethik* which would make us adopt courses of action dictated by a belief in the shortness of time remaining in this age. The blessed hope of the possibly imminent Second Coming should inspire us to more holiness and more consecrated Christian service.

CHAPTER EIGHT

DISPENSATIONALISM

IN THE nineteenth century in England, the Plymouth Brethren started a new method of interpreting Scripture, known as dispensationalism or dispensational truth. Two of the prominent exponents were John Nelson Darby and E. W. Bullinger, so the terms Darbyism and Bullingerism are also used. It has been widely circulated in the notes of the Scofield Reference Bible. A mass of literature has grown up on the subject, so it will be impossible for us to do more than give a brief survey of some of the more important aspects of the subject.

Dispensationalism should be kept clearly distinguished from premillenarianism. All dispensationalists are premillenarians, but there are many premillenarians who are not dispensationalists. Premillenarianism is one of the ancient theories that have been held by Christians down through the ages. Dispensationalists try to claim some of the ancient theologians for their point of view, but the distinctive tenets of dispensationalism cannot be found earlier than the nineteenth century. Premillenarianism is one of the theories of interpreting a certain part of the Bible; whereas dispensationalism places such a distinctive interpretation on the whole Bible that it makes it a new book. The dispensationalists delight in making that claim for their principles; most Christians, however, prefer to keep the old Book and the old principles of interpretation that have come down through the ages.

Large numbers of Christians have used the Scofield Reference Bible with great profit. It does have many splendid features, and certain definite dangers and errors. Those who use it should recognize that Dr. Scofield was both a premillenarian and a dispensationalist, so all of his notes reflect those points of view; a student who understands those theories can make allowances for them. The notes are so brief that they are only dogmatic statements, so the untrained student may easily get the impression that these theories are certain facts. The Scofield Bible may be used with great profit by discerning students, but it is somewhat dangerous to give to the average Bible student.

There is a kind of dispensationalism that is perfectly Scriptural, one that simply distinguishes between certain differences in emphasis before the coming of Christ and after it, the old covenant and the new, the old testament and the new, law and grace. But this view teaches clearly that God has always saved men only by grace, only because of the merit of the death of the Saviour, and only upon the condition of faith. But the new dispensationalism is something quite different. In speaking of dispensationalism we shall use the term to apply to the beliefs of the Plymouth Brethren and their modern followers.

A dispensation is supposed to be a certain period of time during which God dealt with man in respect to his obedience of a certain specific revelation of the will of God. There are said to be seven such dispensations in Scripture. Scofield names them and describes them in connection with the following passages: 1. Innocency, Genesis 1:28; 2. Conscience, Genesis 3:23; 3. Human Government, Genesis 8:20; 4. Promise, Genesis 12:1; 5. Law, Exodus 19:8; 6. Grace, John 1:17; and 7. Kingdom, Ephesians 1:10. The first dispensation, innocency, lasted from creation until the fall. Conscience lasted from the fall to the flood. Human government lasted from the flood to Abraham. Promise went from Abraham to Moses. The law held sway from Moses to Calvary. We are now in the dispensation of grace. The dispensation of the kingdom will come at the Second Coming.

It is easy to see, of course, a certain progressiveness in God's dealing with His people which may well be outlined in some such way as this. But the real dispensationalist goes far beyond that, taking positions that differ radically from the standard interpretation of the Bible.

It is very easy to interpret dispensationalism as teaching that there are seven different ways of salvation rather than just one. Some dispensationalists are aware of that danger, and insist that they believe in only one way of salvation; in which case what is

[55]

the purpose of God's testing His people in the different ways? Some dispensationalists, instead of having seven different ways of salvation, swing back and forth between two, law and grace. That is better than seven, though Scripture seems to indicate clearly that the only person who was ever saved by law was the God-man Himself, our Saviour. If a person wishes to be a dispensationalist he should be far more careful than most of the dispensationalists in making it clear that he believes in only one effective way of salvation, by grace through faith; anything else is heresy of the most dangerous sort. As the dispensationalists say that we are now in the dispensation of grace and that salvation now is by grace through faith, for practical purposes their views do not do so much harm at this point.

But they take an erroneous view of law that does have a great deal of practical importance. We are no longer in the dispensation of law, so the law has no real meaning for us; we are not bound by its provisions, its study is of no benefit to us. Thus they become anti-nomians. The Scriptural view of the law, however, is very different. Law has never been a means of salvation except for the person who could keep it perfectly, and only our Saviour was ever able to do that. The law was given to show man how sinful he really was and how he needed salvation from the penalty of a broken law; it was given to be a schoolmaster to lead the sinner to the Saviour. Then the sinner is saved by faith in Jesus Christ. Is he through with the law then? Not at all. The law is still the will of God. And now that the sinner has become a child of God through faith in Jesus, he wishes to learn how to be a good child of such a Father. The law becomes his guide so that he may grow in holiness. The Christian seeks to keep the law, not hoping to gain his salvation thereby, but seeking to bring forth good fruits, to show his gratitude to God, to become in a measure worthy of the high calling of sons of God. Not for one moment should a Christian despise the law of God; he should give to it just the place that Scripture gives to it.

The dispensationalists tend to divide Scripture into seven watertight compartments. We in the sixth dispensation have a right to claim only a certain part for ourselves, roughly the book of Acts and the Epistles. Such great things as the Ten Commandments, the Sermon on the Mount, and the Lord's Prayer are not for us at all. The dispensationalists claim to be very conservative in their theology, but in effect they are very radical, taking away from us about six-sevenths of all of Scripture. Yes, dispensationalism makes the Bible a new book; but most Christians believe that it makes it not a better one but one infinitely smaller and poorer.

Dispensationalists make a great distinction between the Kingdom of God and the Kingdom of Heaven, whereas a study of a harmony of the Gospels shows clearly that those terms are interchangeable. Mark and Luke use the term Kingdom of God, while Matthew usually uses the other term in reporting exactly the same teaching, using a synonym for God in accordance with a Jewish feeling that the name of God should be pronounced as seldom as possible.

The dispensationalists deny that the Church and the Kingdom have anything to do with one another. Christ came to offer the Kingdom to Israel, but when it was rejected, the age of the Church came in as a kind of parenthesis. It is hard to see how this can be harmonized with the unchanging purposes of God. And such a view makes it necessary to give a very strange interpretation to many of the Biblical teachings about the Kingdom. Actually the Biblical concept of the Kingdom is a broad one. In one sense there is a bit of the Kingdom in the heart of every believer, as God reigns over his life. In one sense the Kingdom is the Church; we see it growing, like a seed growing into a great tree, like leaven gradually permeating the whole lump; we see the wheat and the tares growing side by side; and we see some members bringing forth much fruit, some little, and some none. Some Christians believe that there will be a millenarian phase of the Kingdom. Then there will be the final phase, when the Kingdom will come in all its fulness.

In dealing with the future, all of the dispensationalists are premillenarians, and most of them believe that they are able to make very full and exact charts of the last days. As we have seen, premillenarianism is one of the good theories of the Church, but it may become dangerous when it is presented as a fact rather than a theory and when its advocates become too dogmatic about the details of elaborate charts.

Most Christians believe that modern dispensationalism has nothing whatever of value to add to the ancient Christian use of the Bible but rather that it has certain points of very real danger, points that strike at some of the fundamentals of the creeds of the historic, evangelical Churches.

CHAPTER NINE

THE GREAT PYRAMID AND THE ANGLO-ISRAEL THEORY

~~~~~~

EVERYONE knows something about the mighty pyramids of Egypt. The largest of them, known as the Great Pyramid, one of those located at Gizeh, was considered one of the seven wonders of the ancient world. Until very recent times it was the tallest and largest building ever made by man. As an architectural and engineering feat it is still amazing. The orientation is exceedingly exact. Originally it was covered with a coat of highly polished stone, so it must have been a magnificent sight under the brilliant sun.

The other pyramids were built as tombs, and it is highly probable that this one was built as the tomb of Cheops, a pharaoh of the Fourth Dynasty, otherwise known as Khufu. The sarcophagus in the chamber known as the King's Chamber is empty, but that is probably due to an early rifling of the tomb.

In very recent times a school of thought has arisen which believes that this Great Pyramid is in reality a storehouse of prophecy. In ancient times the architect received a revelation from God foretelling the course of events from creation to the end of this age. Down through the ages that was sealed up, and now in the last days it has been discovered and made known to those who are wise enough to understand it.

Nowhere in the pyramid is there any writing saying that a certain thing would happen at a certain time. How, then, do the pyramid students get their predictions? It is by a curious mixture of architecture, mathematics, astronomy, history, and prophecy. We cannot go into the manifold details, but let us look at some of their methods and results.

They get their starting point by drawing a line down along the original outer coating and another line down what is known as the ascending passage. Down below the surface of the earth these two lines will intersect. That intersection is taken to be the starting point. It is said that the pyramid and Scripture prove that the world was created in the year 4000 B. C. Anyone who has made anything of a study of Biblical chronology knows something of the problems involved, of the gaps that must be filled in by theory, of the problem of the differences between the Hebrew and the Greek manuscripts, and so on; Scripture certainly does not prove 4000 B. C. Archbishop Ussher long ago guessed 4004 B. C. Many students of Scripture believe that the great ages of geology may be in perfect harmony with Scripture. But the pyramidists are quite certain that 4000 B. C. was the beginning.

In the antechamber there is a horseshoe-shaped stone almost exactly an inch thick. This thickness is taken to be the "pyramid inch," and it is then taken to mean one year. Then suddenly its value changes and becomes one month, as the pyramid is supposed to predict in greater detail the events of the last days before the end.

From the zero year point you must go up the imaginary line until you reach the ascending passage and go on up until you reach the level of the antechamber and the King's Chamber. The line from the zero year point to the top of the ascending passage is called the plane of recorded prophecies. The top level is the "plane of time of the end."

Now if you will drop a line from the main entrance in the north side of the pyramid it will cross the line of the recorded prophecies at a certain point. Counting up from the zero year point by pyramid inches, we see the remarkable fact that the pyramid predicted that in 2345 and 2344 B. C. the flood would occur. Of course Bible students are not able to give such exact dates for such early events, but the pyramidists are able to get the dates most exactly from the pyramid. How was the flood predicted? In reality that seems to have been about the only major event that took place at about that time.

Where the prophetic line intersects the base line is taken to be a prediction of the call of Abraham. The junction of the ascending and the descending passages gives the prediction of the exodus, so the pyramidists are now able to give an exact date to that event that has given rise to so many theories on the part of Biblical scholars and archaeologists. Where the prophetic line comes to the passage leading to the Queen's Chamber we are able to see predictions of the birth of Christ, His ministry, and His death and resurrection. And at long last we are able to give exact dates for all those events. He was born October 6, 4 B. C. He began His ministry when He was baptized by John on October 3, 27 A. D. His ministry lasted two and a half years, exactly 918 days and one hour. His crucifixion took place April 7, 30 A. D.

From that point on up the roof of the ascending passage is much higher, so the passage is called the Grand Gallery. This is supposed to be a prediction of the Christian era. Now if one will only examine the condition of the stones that line the wall near the floor of the Grand Gallery he will be able to see predictions of the whole course of Church history. Where the stones are in good condition, there is strength in the Church; where they are rough and scarred, there is weakness. Thus the pyramid predicted the first 400 years of strength and purity in the Church, the invasion of the Goths, the hegira of the prophet Mohammed, the defeat of the Mohammedans at Tours in 732, the degradation of the Catholic Church, the Reformation, and so on. At the point for the year 1844 we come to the Great Step; thus the pyramid predicted the beginning of the mechanical age but an age when spiritual progress did not go along with the physical.

At the edge of the Great Step the pyramid inch changes its value and becomes one month. At the point for August 4-5, 1914, we come to a low passage; thus the pyramid predicted the beginning of World War I (the date when England entered it). The low passage ends at the point standing for November 9-10, 1918, so we see the end of the war (when the Kaiser abdicated and fled).

Then we come into the antechamber, where the ceiling is high and we find relief from the low passage. Going through the antechamber we come to a second low passage, which gives us a prediction that there would be a world-wide depression which would begin on May 29, 1928. That low passage comes to an end at the point for September 16, 1936, and we move into the grand King's Chamber. Thus it was predicted that man's final tribulation, the great depression, would come to an end at that definite date, that Christ would return and lead His people into the glories of His millennial kingdom. The pyramidists made a great deal of that day as it approached. Now it has come and gone. World War II is here, and there are no more low passages. We may be sure that their ingenuity will find a way to explain and make new prophecies.

We have followed simply the main features of the main line, but any good pyramidist can see many symbolic messages throughout the pyramid.

What can we say of all of this pseudo-science? We may say very bluntly that there is absolutely nothing in it. It is unthinkable that God should have made His predictions in any such way as that. Of what value is a prediction if it cannot be understood until after the event supposedly predicted? Who would ever have dreamed that the union of two imaginary lines constituted a prediction of the flood? By handling dates very freely a pyramid student can see many "predictions" of events that have already occurred. A writer in 1934 made very accurate predictions of events up until that time. The only real predictions were those after 1934; and September 16, 1936, which was set as the end of this age, has come and gone, and Christ has not brought in His millennial kingdom yet.

There is nothing whatever in Scripture that would indicate that God would ever make such a revelation. The pyramidists quote Jeremiah 32:18-20 as a kind of Scriptural background: "The Great, the Mighty God . . . hast set signs and wonders in the land of Egypt, even unto this day." But Jeremiah never dreamed about any such thing as prophetic values of the Great Pyramid. The pyramidists add to the prophecies of Scripture; do they merit the curse of Revelation for those "who add to the words of the prophecy of this book"?

Even in dealing with past events, it is strange that the pyramid predicted just those events that it did, overlooking many events far more significant than many of those predicted. The fact is, of course, that when the pyramidists could find any justification for any date, at the intersection of any of their lines or the change in condition of the stones or the change in the height of the passages, they looked around in history and got some event that could be dated approximately at that time; then they say that the pyramid has proved that that is the exact date for the event.

Many, if not most, of the pyramidists hold to the Anglo-Israel theory. They think that the ten lost tribes are the English and American peoples today. Therefore, we of Anglo-Saxon descent have the right to claim, along with the Jews, all of the promises that God made to His ancient people.

They have many "proofs" for their theory. By disregarding the laws of etymology, which is a rather exact science, they are able to see the connection between places and persons among the Israelites and those in England and America today. In its "prediction" for the beginning of World War I, the pyramid predicted the entrance of England rather than the actual beginning. The great seal of the United States actually has a pyramid on its reverse side. Such "proofs" can be multiplied indefinitely.

There is just about as much logic in the Anglo-Israel theory as in that of the prophetic value of the Great Pyramid—none whatever.

It is not known just what happened when the Northern Kingdom was captured. There was something of a deportation. Some of the people seem to have stayed in the land and have intermarried with the surrounding peoples. Those who were taken away did pass off the pages of Scripture. They were probably assimilated by their captors. If they did keep their identity, where they are now is a complete mystery to all of us. Many guesses have been made. Each guesser is always sure that he himself is one of the Israelites.

Scripture itself makes absolutely nothing of the "ten lost tribes." In fact, the New Testament makes it plain that the important thing is to be a spiritual Jew rather than a literal one. The promises are to be inherited by the spiritual, rather than the literal, children af Abraham, by those who have his faith rather than his blood. The Anglo-Israelites neglect these plain teachings of the New Testament and place a very literal interpretation on many of the passages of the Bible where it is completely unnecessary or is even out of harmony with the real context.

CHAPTER TEN

THE CULTS

WE HAVE attempted to emphasize primarily the things that Scripture teaches clearly about the future, then to see some of the better theories of interpreting those parts of Scripture that are not so clear, and then, finally, to see some of the fanciful and fantastic views that are commonly held which are out of harmony with Scripture at important points. There are many, many cults and sects that teach strange and unscriptural views about the future; we shall call attention to a few of the typical ones in conclusion.

One of the sects, the Mormons, was founded in the early nineteenth century by an American, Joseph Smith, who claimed to have received a new revelation from God that had been recorded on golden plates, to which he had been miraculously directed by an angel, and which he claims to have translated by means of a pair of supernatural spectacles. This book becomes a supplement to Scripture for the members of the sect; for practical purposes it is to them more important than the Bible itself. Then the presidents of the sect have the power to receive new revelations from God from time to time, so gradually the cult drifts further and further from Biblical teachings. For a time the cultists practiced polygamy. Now that that can no longer be done legally, the leaders urge the members to abide by the laws of the land; yet they still believe in it and look forward to the time when it may be practiced again, in heaven if not on earth.

The Mormons believe in celestial marriage. Husband and wife are married for eternity. A woman cannot attain the highest bliss in heaven unless she is married, so men should take pity on women and marry as many of them as possible. Heaven itself is to be a place of endless, aimless procreation, surely a far cry from the beautiful, pure pictures of heaven found in Scripture.

The Mormons hold to a kind of premillenarianism. Each of the two branches of the sect has picked out a city which will be the New Jerusalem—Salt Lake City, Utah, and Independence, Missouri. They believe that the millennium will practice a kind of socialistic living, so they are making attempts to put as much of that into practice as possible now, but without much success, even where there are large numbers of the cultists living together.

Another more modern sect, that of the Jehovah's Witnesses, or Russellites, or International Bible Students Association, was founded by another American who died early in the twentieth century, Pastor Russell; he was succeeded by Judge Rutherford. This cult claims an intense loyalty to the Bible, and all of their abundant literature is full of Bible quotations. This cult is an illustration of the well-known fact that you can prove anything out of the Bible if you are willing to twist it around to your own purposes. The members of this sect are uniformly persons who have had no training whatever in a scholarly interpretation of the Bible; most of them have had little education of any kind. They readily follow the fanciful interpretations of the founder and his successors, and they have an intense hatred of the regular Christian Churches, especially the clergy and the theological seminary professors.

The Witnesses do not believe in the reality of hell as a place of eternal torment. They do not believe in the immortality of the soul. When a man dies he has existence only in the memory of God. At the resurrection, some at least will come back to life.

This cult, too, believes in a kind of premillenarianism. The founder in 1914 said that Jesus would come again that year. When the year passed, instead of admitting his mistake, he developed the view that Christ did come and throw Satan out of heaven. Now Jesus is in the air, for some reason delaying the actual setting up of His millennial reign. They are quite sure that "millions now living will never die." Soon the battle of Armageddon will be fought between the forces of Satan, especially the Satanic Churches, and the small band of the true forces of Christ, the 144,000, the members of the cult, of course.

[66]

During the millennium, Christ and the members of the cult will reign in the air. The people who have not become true believers before will have another chance during the thousand years. First God will work with those who were still alive at the beginning of the period. Then the dead will begin to come forth, a few at a time, and will have all the rest of the millennium to get right with God. Those who do not respond to the second chance and who follow Satan when he is released at the end of the millennium will be annihilated like Satan himself. So everyone—except probably the preachers and seminary professors—will have another chance to escape hell; and those who fail a second time will be simply blotted out. What a comforting belief —for sinners!

The Seventh-Day Adventists likewise teach the soul-sleep after death and the final annihilation of the wicked. The founder of the sect, Miller, predicted that Christ would come again in 1843, and all of his followers got their white robes ready to meet the Lord. When that date passed, he discovered the error of his figures and said that he was absolutely certain that He would come on October 22, 1844. When that day passed, he gave up, but some of the faithful did not; they developed the theory that Jesus had come on that day and had entered into the inner sanctuary of the temple to complete His work of atonement—as though that had not been done on Calvary!

Spiritualism is a cult that has had its ups and downs. From the earliest times men have been trying to find some way to gain contact with those who have died. They wish to obtain comfort and also to get supernatural insight into the future. The Bible teaches, of course, that the dead live on. But it does not teach that they can come back and tell us about themselves and tell us what the future holds in store for us. But the "mediums" claim to be able to get in contact with the spirits of our dead friends and loved ones. By means of predetermined codes of table rappings and other such phenomena, messages may be obtained. The spirits work best, of course, in dark rooms; they usually refuse to work at all when doubtful skeptics are there for the purpose of testing them. The Spiritualists have produced a mass of literature, have founded many churches, have won some famous converts. But large numbers of their mediums have been proven conclusively to have been frauds. The Fox sisters, who are the real founders of modern Spiritualism, admitted that all the phenomena were purely natural and that there was nothing to their fraudulent claims; then they later recanted their recantation. The mediums make use of clever magical tricks, but Houdini, who made a serious study of Spiritualism and really tried to accept it, said that he could reproduce every single phenomenon of all of the mediums. Some Christians think that there is some real demonic power at work, though the explanation of pure magic is probably far better.

Intelligent Christians surely do not need to be warned against the trickery of the mind readers, the fortunetellers, the astrologers, and all of their kind who prey upon superstitious persons to this very day. If these charlatans can tell their clients how to make so much money in their business deals, why do they have to live in such poor tents and huts? Some of them employ some rather clever tricks. All of them try to make their answers vague enough to fit any eventuality, using the ancient trick of the Delphic Oracle.

But enough of the roll call of the cults. Time does not permit a description of Theosophy, Bahaism, Unity, Swedenborgianism, and all the rest of the present-day Babel of voices that claim to have a new and better solution for the problems of this life and the one to come.

The cults and isms come and go. Some are started by dishonest people for the purpose of making money; and as man is an incurably religious animal, the cultists have often grown fabulously wealthy. Some of them, though, are started by perfectly honest persons, but persons who do not have a true knowledge of the real teachings of Scripture.

Historic Christianity has lasted through the centuries, and it will last until this age gives way to eternity. The true Church does not know the answer to all the questions about the future, because God has not seen fit to reveal it to us. It is hardly probable, to say the least, that God will make any new special revelation to one of the tiny cults rather than to His own Church.

Every Christian has a right to claim all the comfort and assurance that can come from a true understanding of the revelation of Scripture about the future. Such a knowledge will enable him to make the most of this life and to prepare for the life that is to come. He should be very cautious about accepting anything that claims to be a new and revolutionary insight into the other life or a new interpretation of Scripture that makes void the conclusions of the students of Scripture who have worked down through the centuries.